THE EARLY MORNING MILK TRAIN

THE EARLY MORNING MILK TRAIN

The Cream of Emett Railway Drawings

THE STEPHEN GREENE PRESS
Brattleboro, Vermont

First American Edition, 1977
Published by arrangement with John Murray Ltd.,
50 Albemarle Street, London WIX 4BD

© This selection Rowland Emett 1976
Foreword © Bevis Hillier 1976

The pictures in this book are reproduced
from PUNCH by kind permission
of the Proprietors

Printed in Great Britain by
Fletcher & Son Ltd, Norwich
0-8289-0299-2
Library of Congress catalog card number 76-56665
Bound by The Book Press
Brattleboro, Vermont

FOREWORD BY BEVIS HILLIER

There were three great turning-points in Rowland Emett's life. The first was in 1939, when his researches into the lesser forms of steam transportation began to be revealed by *Punch*. The second was the invitation from James Gardner, chief designer of the Battersea Pleasure Gardens for the Festival of Britain, 1951, to translate the 'Far Twittering and Oyster Creek Railway' of his spidery *Punch* drawings into three dimensions to carry people round the exhibition. This resulted in that extraordinarily whimsical railway system of which the locomotives, Nellie, Neptune and Wildgoose, were compounded of rum barrels, divers' helmets, Cranford tea kettles and other objects of inspired improvisation. On the wittily designed stations were forbidding notices: 'Do NOT tease the engines'; 'WARN-ING: When Red Lobster is hoisted, Tide is OUT'; (at the entrance to a tunnel) 'Do NOT feed the Bats'; and that petulant one – 'Trains cross here, so THERE!'

The success of this system, now burgeoning in three mahogany, brass-bound dimensions brought about another turning-point. Emett was besieged by digni-fied, responsible companies for large, devious machines to promote their interests, and so it was that the drawings (sadly, perhaps) slid gradually out of *Punch*, into a cloud-cuckoo land of high-tension string, bamboo and bicycle wheels. The resulting machines grace many a board-room and now such halls of science as the Smithsonian Institution, the Chicago Museum of Science and Industry, and the Ontario Science Centre.

The social historian and art historian will find in Emett's cartoons much that is typical of that austerity-to-affluence period of the 1940s and 50s. Above all there is the glorification of the individual and the eccentric as an antidote to the regi-mentation and rationing to which the English had had to submit for their own good. The individual standing on his dignity or up for his rights, even when a train has been re-routed through his drawing room, is central to Emett's quizzical vision. He is against lumping-together, pooling of rolling stock, electrification, nationalization, slavish obedience to Rules (the last beautifully sent up in a draw-ing in which two men living Pegotty-like in upturned boats, have compelled a retired engine-driver to 'observe the basic architectural rule of the district' and upturn his locomotive to live in). He is for architectural follies, cantankerous commuters, umbrella-brandishing *grandes dames* and marvels of embroidered engineering. His people are at one with his locomotives – those endearing folk of whom it has been said: 'they are standing about on station platforms, too late for the past and too early for the present'.

I asked Rowland Emett why the locomotive should have been, literally, the vehicle for his fantasies. He replied: 'However could it be otherwise? What more romantic than, say, the late sun burnishing the Afternoon Slow Stopper to St Torpids Creek . . . luminous mists up to the axle-boxes, and perhaps first and second seagull obbligato . . .?' I also asked how he saw himself in relation to that other great inventor of self-sufficient railways, Heath Robinson. He pondered a moment and then said 'some years ago the *Sunday Times* did an article to explain me away and wrote: "He is, of course, the Heath Robinson of to-day". Not long ago, in an article on the work of Heath Robinson they neatly tucked in any loose ends by remarking: "He was, of course, the Emett of his day".'

"For all YOU know we might be Clapham Junction."

"*Some footling nonsense about a right of way, or something . . .*"

"... *shan't be sorry when* I *retire* ..."

Hostile elements

Technical hitch at the Official Inauguration

"*I keep* TELLING *him we've done away with First Class!*"

"Bother – it's a smoker!"

*"The train standing at No. 5 platform is the midnight slow for
Spectral Manor, Gallows Hill, Grisly Grange, and Hangdog Heath."*

"... and then they bring out this Pooling of Rolling Stock business."

"*When are you going to see the Directors about a luggage-van?*"

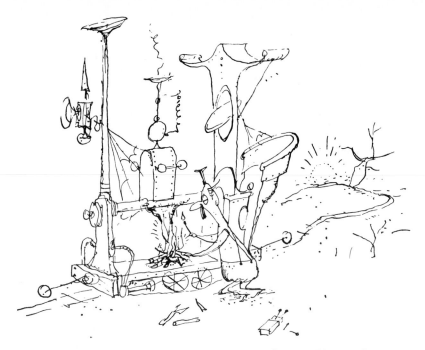

Steam raising, early morning

The Night Sleeper to Oysterperch Bay

"Nothing exciting in the paper this morning, I suppose?"

"*Rabbit, sir?*"

"Takes a bit of getting used to, a spot of holiday traffic."

"Something to do with the nationalization of railways, I expect."

"Ah, THAT'S what I've always said : study the individual . . ."

"*Here's the 9.15. I see they've taken it off.*"

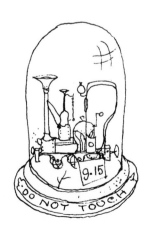

"I wish they'd have their Board Meetings when they GET to Town!"

". . . he says very poor – rub out, do again and see him after six . . ."

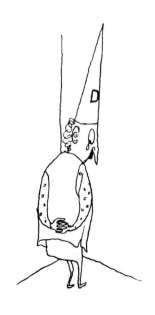

Porter's half-holiday

The Bird Watcher's Special to Twittering Woods

"I should have gone easy with the heat at first."

"Let's see – sail gives way to steam – or is it the other way round?"

". . . and a plaguy great dish o' tay will not come amiss at Brighthelmstone, I'll warrant me."

"*I* STILL *reckon we should have been the 8.35 to the City . . . !*"

". . . something to do with Lease-Lend, I expect . . ."

"*Between you and me, sir, we don't quite know where* THAT *line goes to . . .*"

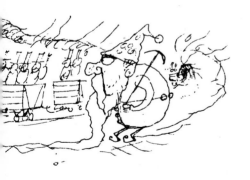

"*. . . and I asked him for two seats facing the engine, and* HE *said well, there's a war on, but he'd see what he could do. . . .*"

"Aye, the Afternoon Slow is always a help with Top Meadow . . ."

A Motorist teasing a train

The Evening Train arriving at Smuggler's Reach.

"... I said : the nights are drawing in quickly now ..."

"*Serving dinner on the trains again, I see.*"

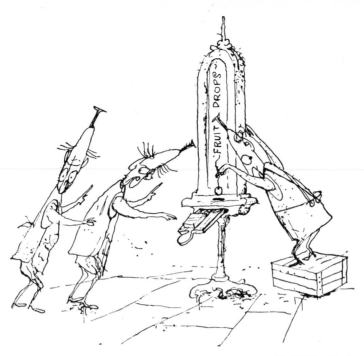

Forbidden Fruit

The Early Morning Milk Train passing the old Cloud Cuckoo Creek tide-mill

"Despite the severe depletion of equipment and rolling stock, the Company will do all in its power to resume meals on the trains."

"*Y-e-s . . . there* WAS *a gale warning on the eight o'clock, but* THAT *was for shipping.*"

"*We feel we ought to do* SOMETHING *to take their minds off* THAT."

"*Can't* ANYBODY *suggest an opening phrase for the third movement?*"

"Salmon or pheasant?"

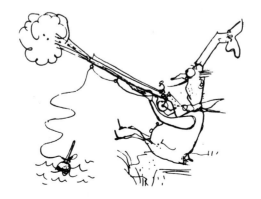

"*I'm* POSITIVE *we didn't have to change the last time.*"

Hector, Nellie and Another

Examples of thoughtfulness for passengers' comfort on parts of system where amenities would otherwise be lacking

"*Ah, yes – chap from London was* TELLING *me the Underground was pushing farther afield.*"

"*I said, that's the proper place for him. After all, he's the captain, in a manner of speaking.*"

"*There you are – that's what they* SAID *they'd do : Railways, Road Services and Canals, all lumped together.*"

"*Psst! Squatters in number three.*"

" 'Electrification', they say: and gone, gone is the wonder and romance of the
Iron Road!"

". . . Until they release the new dining cars, we'll just have to do our best."

"I TOLD *you never to take the 11.50 round by the Witch Hollow loop . . . !"*

Three Porters and a Station-master

Unusual triple disaster at Loambarrow Bottom 👉

"A plague on the 'Devon Belle' and its new glass observation coach."

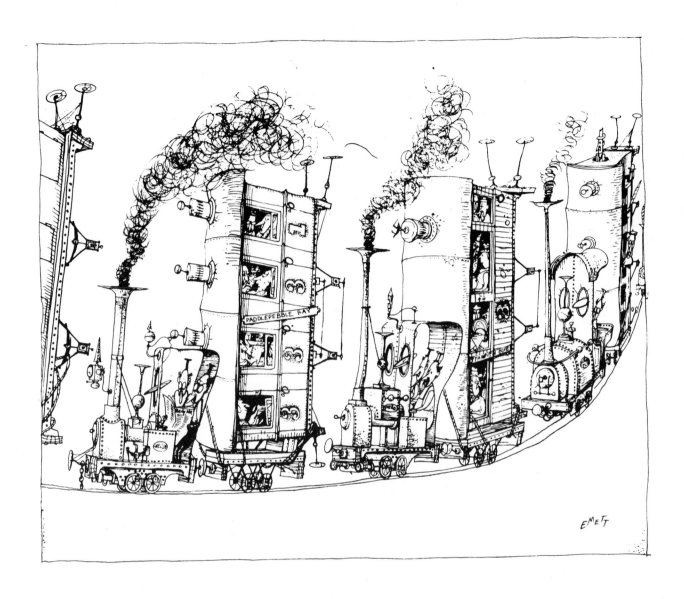

"*Just when we've found a way to crowd more holiday trains on the line – pfft! – ten per cent cut . . . !*"

"*One in the eye for the Coal Board it* MAY *be, but have you thought about the Timber Controller?*"

"*They say very sorry they'll have to have it back, but can offer in exchange desirable old-world property, detached, one up one down, balcony, positive sun-trap . . .*"

". . . and if they draw us into this Railway Nationalization scheme, BANG goes our individuality!"

A Proposed Buffet-car

Pleasing Example of Resource in Emergency on part of personnel 👉

"*Just a dress-rehearsal . . . we're not going to get caught out* THIS *winter . . . !*"

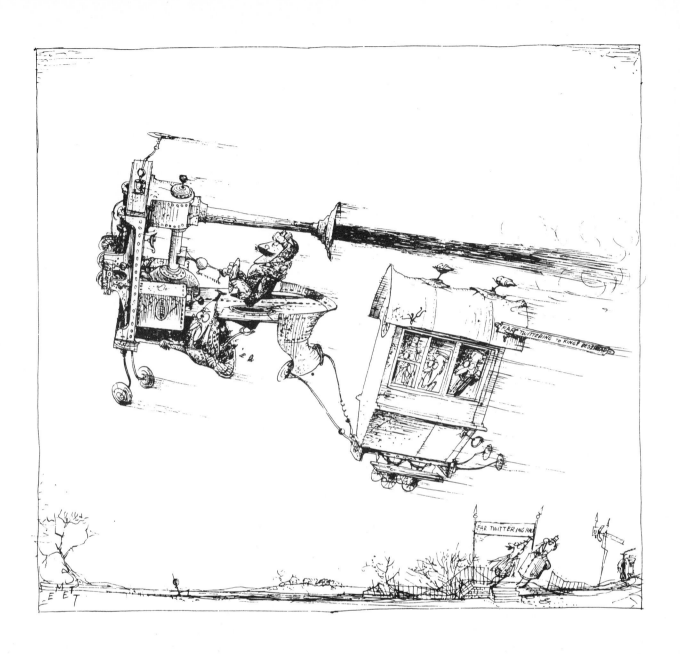

"I'm not at all sure that the Labour Exchange has sent us the right sort of man for our stuff . . ."

"*So they've taken off the 'Cornish Riviera' – I wonder why the eagle eye hasn't dropped on us.*"

"*Granted the trains are slower than they were, and granted they use what rolling stock they can get, I* STILL *think we're in the wrong train.*"

"*Here's someone from the Government wants to see about making us part of the Network . . .*"

"Some established institutions are BOUND *to get topsy-turvy with the march of science . . ."*

"*Ah, yes . . . I read somewhere the railways were to give up using horses . . .*"

"Oh well . . . ! season of mists and mellow fruitfulness . . ."

Monday morning

Example of fuel economy method in operation

"*None of them could make up their minds* HOW *they wanted their engine painted . . .*"

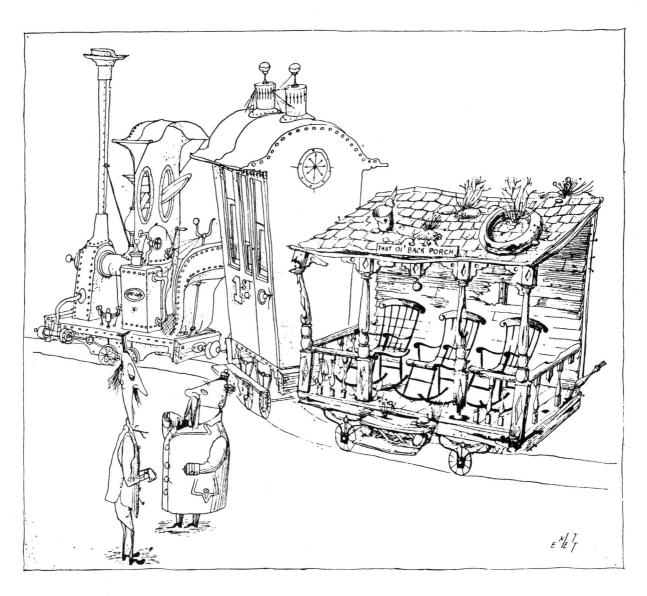

"*Yes, we're making a* SPECIAL *bid for the American tourist business this summer* . . ."

" 'Freak Magnetic Storm' the papers'll have it this evening . . ."

"There you are, you see – a failing concern can always be revived with a spot of showmanship . . ."

"Anyhow, we compelled him to observe the basic architectural rule of the district . . ."

"... *with fares as they are, we're beginning to find we've got to* TEMPT *them* ..."

Some passengers

Device used on exposed section to avoid the blowing-over of trains with possible consequent damage

"Keep it under your hat, but I'M *running on red petrol . . .!"**

* *Red petrol was given to those whose driving was essential to the war effort.
It was dyed red to help in detecting its misuse.*

"Yes, I've heard of LOTS *of happily retired chaps being suddenly dragged back into harness . . ."*

"... but I do wish the Housing Committee and the Railway Extension people could have co-ordinated their plans!"

"*You know, Fred, I rather enjoy the lodging turn.*"

"A plague on these new double-deckers . . ."

"I've heard of foreign visitors bringing their own CARS over, but . . ."

Two Drivers despising a Fireman

Locomotive No. 3 (Hector) at Mrs. Bristow's Folly, now used as a water-tower 👉

"Winter service started, I see."

"*And now perhaps a quick word from Driver Firebrace, who is determined that the Yuletide mail shall get through on time . . .*"

"*Oh, you've seen the posters . . . 'Fast Excursions to Dogfish Bay, Trip round Lighthouse, and Winkle Tea, Inclusive 7s. 6d.' . . .*"

"*I* MUST *say they've improved the service* ENORMOUSLY *this year . . .*"

"Well, what d'you think of that! 'No more double-decker trains to be built' . . ."

"*Thank* GOODNESS *the kids have finally gone back to school . . . !*"

"*Actually I'm* GLAD *we couldn't get a sleeper . . .*"

"Ladies and gentlemen, it gives me the greatest pleasure to see amongst us all once again this old and valued friend . . ."

First Returns

Mr. William Funnell's final gesture of defiance in the face of Nationalisation

The end of the line